Applications of Cloud Computing in Enhancing Supply Chain Efficiency for the Agro-Industry

Dr. Alfredo Tutuhatunewa
Prof. Surachman
Purnomo B. Santoso, Ph.D
Prof. Imam Santoso

Department of Industrial Engineering, Faculty of Engineering, Pattimura University

Copyright © 2024, Alfredo Tutuhatunewa, et al.
ISBN: 9798301039430

ACKNOWLEDGEMENTS

We would like to express our deepest gratitude to Pattimura University, particularly the Faculty of Engineering, for their unwavering support and encouragement throughout the development of this book. Their dedication to advancing research and innovation in engineering and technology has been a continuous source of motivation for our team.

Our sincere appreciation also goes to Brawijaya University, where several of our team members pursued their doctoral studies. The faculty and administration at Brawijaya University provided essential guidance and resources that have greatly shaped our research focus and academic growth. We are especially grateful to our mentors and colleagues there, who have inspired us to explore new dimensions in supply chain management and cloud computing applications within the agro-industry.

We are thankful to our colleagues and students at Pattimura University for their valuable insights and discussions, which have enriched our understanding and helped refine the concepts presented in this book. Their enthusiasm and curiosity have pushed us to delve deeper into the practical challenges faced by Micro and Small Enterprises (MSEs) in Indonesia's agricultural sector.

Lastly, we extend our heartfelt thanks to our families and friends for their constant support and patience throughout this journey. Their belief in our work has been a source of strength and motivation during the many long hours spent on research and writing.

This book is a result of collaboration, encouragement, and shared knowledge. We are deeply grateful to everyone who has contributed to making this work possible.

Alfredo Tutuhatunewa
Surachman
Purnomo B. Santoso
Imam Santoso

Table of Contents

ACKNOWLEDGEMENTS 2
   Alfredo Tutuhatunewa Surachman 3
CHAPTER I: INTRODUCTION 7
   1.1 Background of Study 7
   1.2 Problem Statement 8
   1.3 Objectives of the Study 10
   1.4 Importance and Relevance of the Model 11
   1.5 Structure of the Monograph 12
CHAPTER II: SUPPLY CHAIN MANAGEMENT IN THE 15
   2.1 Definition and History of Supply Chain Management 15
   2.2 Supply Chain Management in Horticulture 16
   2.3 Key Success Factors in Supply Chain Management 18
CHAPTER III: CLOUD COMPUTING TECHNOLOGY 22
   3.1 Overview of Cloud Computing 22
   3.2 Service Models: SaaS, PaaS, and IaaS 24
      1. Software as a Service (SaaS) 24
      2. Platform as a Service (PaaS) 25
      3. Infrastructure as a Service (IaaS) 26
      Summary of Service Model Benefits 27
CHAPTER IV: APPROACH TO DEVELOPING THE SUPPLY CHAIN MODEL ... 29
   4.1 Approach and Methods 29
      1. Research Design 29
      2. Data Collection Techniques 29
      3. Sampling Methods 30
      5. Development of the Cloud-Based Model 31
      6. Evaluation Metrics 31
   4.2 Selecting Participants for Model Development 32
      1. Targeted Selection of Key Supply Chain Actors 32
      2. Engagement of Accessible Participants 33

3. Diversity of Business Roles and Perspectives 33
4.3 Gathering and Understanding Data 34
    1. Information Gathering from Supply Chain Participants 34
    2. Examining Patterns and Key Themes 35
    3. Using Insights to Shape the Model 35
4.4 Scope and Considerations 36
    1. Geographical and Participant Scope 36
    2. Sample Size and Representation 37
    3. Dependence on Self-Reported Data 37
    4. Technological Adoption and Readiness 37
    5. Evolving Market and Environmental Conditions 38

CHAPTER V: INSIGHTS INTO THE APPLE AGRO-INDUSTRY SUPPLY CHAIN 39

5.1 Characteristics of MSEs in the Apple Agro-Industry 39
    1. Diverse Product Offerings 39
    2. Seasonal and Perishable Nature of Raw Materials 39
    3. Resource Constraints and Limited Economies of Scale 40
    4. Reliance on Conventional Markets and Distribution Channels 40
    5. Challenges in Supply Chain Coordination and Communication 40
    6. Low Adoption of Digital and Cloud-Based Tools 41
    7. Adaptability and Innovation in Response to Market Needs 41
5.2 Supplier and Distributor Relations 41
    1. Dependence on Local Suppliers for Raw Materials 42
    2. Procurement and Payment Practices 42
    3. Coordination with Distributors and Retailers 43
    4. Communication Challenges 44
    5. Opportunities for Improvement with Cloud-Based Solutions 45
5.3 Challenges in the Apple Agro-Industry Supply Chain 46
    1. Resource Constraints and Limited Scale 46

2. Complexities in Supplier Relations 47
   3. Market Access and Distribution Constraints 47
   4. Manual and Inefficient Processes 48
   5. Coordination and Transparency Across the Supply Chain . 49
   6. Limited Technological Adoption 49

CHAPTER VI: DEVELOPMENT OF A CLOUD-BASED SUPPLY CHAIN MODEL 51
   6.1 Model Overview and Components 51
      Model Overview 51
      Key Components of the Model 52
   6.2 Information Flow and Practical Applications 55
      Information Flow in the Supply Chain Model 55
      Practical Applications of the Model 56
      1. Optimizing Inventory Management 56
      2. Automating Order Processing 57
      3. Enhancing Supplier Coordination 57
      4. Using Demand Forecasting to Plan Production 57
      5. Monitoring Supply Chain Performance and Making
         Adjustments 58
   6.3 Benefits and Challenges of Implementing Cloud Solutions ... 58
      Benefits of Cloud Implementation 58
      Challenges of Cloud Implementation 61

CHAPTER VII: FINAL INSIGHTS AND FUTURE OPPORTUNITIES 64
   7.1 Key Takeaways 64
   7.2 Implications for the Agro-Industry 66
   7.3 Looking Ahead: Suggestions for Future Development 69
      Summary 72

REFERENCES 73
ABOUT THE AUTHOR 77

CHAPTER I: INTRODUCTION

1.1 Background of Study

Micro and Small Enterprises (MSEs) hold a strategic role in many national economies, particularly in emerging markets, due to their contribution to employment and local economic resilience. In Indonesia, for example, MSEs contribute significantly to employment, supporting over 11 million jobs as recorded by the Department of Cooperatives and Micro, Small, and Medium Enterprises in East Java (Hill, 2001). Despite their important role, MSEs face numerous challenges that impede their growth, including limited access to resources and markets, lack of economies of scale, and an underdeveloped information infrastructure (Yoshino & Taghizadeh-Hesary, 2016). The apple agro-industry in Batu City, East Java, is a pertinent example, where local MSEs engaged in apple processing encounter these very challenges.

In the context of a globalized and competitive market, achieving efficiency and responsiveness in the supply chain becomes essential for MSEs. The growing emphasis on consumer demand, product quality, and quick response to market changes has pressured MSEs to develop innovative strategies to remain competitive (Simpson et al., 2004). For the apple agro-industry, managing the supply chain efficiently can lead to improved production processes, cost reduction, and enhanced product quality, directly influencing the competitive advantage of these enterprises customers (Skintzi, 2007).

One approach to strengthening the supply chain for MSEs is by leveraging advancements in technology, particularly cloud computing. Cloud computing has gained popularity due to its potential to enhance operational efficiency and data management capabilities. The technology provides flexible, scalable solutions for information sharing and collaboration among different actors in the supply chain, including suppliers, producers, and distributors (Sinha, 2013). By integrating a cloud-based supply chain information system, MSEs can overcome some of the barriers to growth, such as limited access to information and insufficient collaboration across the supply chain (Kochan et al., 2018).

The need for a robust supply chain information system tailored for MSEs in the apple agro-industry in Batu City is evident. A cloud-based model offers a viable solution for addressing core issues like limited market access, high dependency on conventional markets, and challenges in accessing up-to-date market and supply information. A model that uses both Platform as a Service (PaaS) and Software as a Service (SaaS) can offer a sustainable platform for MSEs to improve data accessibility, inventory management, and customer satisfaction, ultimately boosting their competitiveness (Priyadarshinee et al., 2017).

The background of this study underscores the significance of developing a supply chain information system based on cloud computing technology for MSEs in the apple agro-industry. The implementation of such a system aligns with the broader goals of increasing efficiency, enhancing product quality, and fostering competitive advantage in the agro-industry sector.

1.2 Problem Statement

Micro and Small Enterprises (MSEs) in the apple agro-industry, especially in regions like Batu City, East Java, face numerous structural and operational obstacles. These enterprises often struggle with limited access to resources, fluctuating raw material prices, and an underdeveloped supply chain infrastructure.

The apple agro-industry is hindered by challenges in managing the flow of information, goods, and finances among key players—suppliers, producers, and distributors. Consequently, MSEs in this industry find it difficult to maintain efficiency, responsiveness, and consistency in meeting consumer demands.

One primary issue is the reliance on conventional, manual methods for managing supply chain operations. Many MSEs lack the tools necessary for real-time data access and sharing, which are crucial for adapting to market changes and consumer expectations. As a result, processes such as inventory management, product pricing, and order fulfillment are inefficient, often leading to high costs, delayed deliveries, and inconsistent product quality. This lack of coordination impedes the capacity of MSEs to create competitive products that meet market standards.

Additionally, the absence of a structured information network complicates collaboration among supply chain actors. Without effective information sharing, MSEs are unable to forecast demand accurately, manage inventories optimally, or coordinate efficiently with suppliers and distributors. In an increasingly competitive and fast-paced market, this disconnect places MSEs at a significant disadvantage.

The challenge, therefore, is to develop a model that not only addresses these operational gaps but also empowers MSEs to leverage technological advancements, such as cloud computing, for better supply chain integration. A cloud-based information system could provide a streamlined, scalable platform for real-time data access, inventory control, and communication across the supply chain. Such a system holds the potential to enhance collaboration, reduce operational costs, and improve overall productivity within the apple agro-industry.

1.3 Objectives of the Study

The objectives of this study are formulated to address the challenges faced by Micro and Small Enterprises (MSEs) in the apple agro-industry supply chain. These objectives aim to establish a technological foundation that will enable these enterprises to enhance their supply chain operations and overall competitiveness. The objectives are as follows:

1. To develop a cloud-based supply chain information system model that can improve information accessibility, inventory management, and coordination among MSEs, suppliers, and distributors within the apple agro-industry.
2. To evaluate the effectiveness of Platform as a Service (PaaS) and Software as a Service (SaaS) as components of a scalable and flexible information system that supports the unique needs of MSEs in managing real-time data, tracking inventory, and streamlining operations.
3. To enhance collaboration capabilities within the apple agro-industry supply chain, enabling MSEs to establish better relationships with suppliers and distributors, improve order fulfillment, and adapt more swiftly to market demands.
4. To analyze the impact of an integrated supply chain information system on the operational efficiency of MSEs, specifically in terms of reducing production costs, minimizing delays, and ensuring product quality.
5. To provide a sustainable model that supports MSEs in developing a competitive edge through effective supply chain management, leveraging cloud computing to improve market access, data sharing, and overall productivity.

By achieving these objectives, the study aims to empower MSEs in the apple agro-industry to operate more effectively and competitively, with a supply chain model that is adaptable, cost-efficient, and technologically advanced.

1.4 Importance and Relevance of the Model

The development of a cloud-based supply chain information system model for the apple agro-industry holds considerable importance for both local businesses and the broader agricultural sector. This initiative is especially relevant for Micro and Small Enterprises (MSEs) that are the backbone of this industry, as it provides them with the tools and capabilities needed to compete in an increasingly digital and interconnected marketplace. The significance and potential impacts of this model are outlined as follows:

1. Enhancing Operational Efficiency: By integrating cloud computing into the supply chain, MSEs can streamline key processes such as inventory management, data sharing, and order processing. This improvement leads to reduced production costs, quicker response times, and a more reliable workflow across all stages of the supply chain.
2. Supporting Local Economic Growth: The apple agro-industry contributes to employment and economic activity in regions like Batu City, East Java. Strengthening MSEs within this sector helps foster local economic resilience by enabling these businesses to operate more competitively, maintain stable employment, and potentially expand into new markets.
3. Empowering Small Enterprises with Technology: Introducing a cloud-based system makes advanced information technology accessible and affordable for small businesses. This model empowers MSEs to operate on par with larger companies by providing tools for real-time data access, flexible scaling, and collaboration—advantages that were previously beyond their reach.
4. Promoting Sustainability in Supply Chain Operations: A well-organized supply chain supported by cloud technology

helps reduce waste and optimize resource use, as MSEs can better match supply with demand and avoid overproduction. This sustainable approach aligns with growing consumer awareness and demand for eco-friendly practices in production and logistics.
5. Establishing a Model for Future Agro-Industries: The proposed cloud-based supply chain information system can serve as a scalable and adaptable framework for other agro-industries beyond apple processing. It offers a practical example of how cloud technology can revolutionize small-scale agricultural supply chains, setting a precedent for similar sectors aiming to modernize their operations.

In essence, this model is relevant for fostering competitive growth, technological empowerment, and sustainable practices within the agro-industry. It provides a pathway for MSEs to overcome traditional limitations and achieve a higher level of productivity and market alignment.

1.5 Structure of the Monograph

This monograph is organized into seven chapters, each presenting a detailed exploration of a cloud-based supply chain information system for Micro and Small Enterprises (MSEs) in the apple agro-industry. The structure is as follows:

- Chapter I: Introduction
  This chapter introduces the context of the study, outlining the challenges that MSEs in the apple agro-industry face, such as limited market access and inefficient supply chain management. It also explains the purpose, importance, and goals of establishing a cloud-based information system to enhance efficiency and competitiveness in this sector.

- Chapter II: Supply Chain Management in the Agro-Industry
  This chapter provides an overview of supply chain management concepts relevant to the agro-industry, focusing on the unique characteristics of managing a supply chain for agricultural products. It explains essential factors, such as resource optimization, collaboration among supply chain actors, and how these impact MSE performance in horticulture-based industries.
- Chapter III: Cloud Computing Technology
  Here, readers are introduced to cloud computing and its applications in managing business operations. Key service models such as Software as a Service (SaaS) and Platform as a Service (PaaS) are explained, along with their potential for improving data access, communication, and operational flexibility in the supply chain.
- Chapter IV: Approach and Methods
  This chapter explains the steps taken to understand and model the current supply chain for the apple agro-industry. It outlines the methods used for gathering information from MSEs, analyzing the flow of materials and information, and identifying gaps that a cloud-based system could address to improve overall supply chain performance.
- Chapter V: Analysis of the Apple Agro-Industry Supply Chain
  This chapter explores the structure and current practices within the apple agro-industry supply chain. It includes classifications of MSEs by product type, sourcing of raw materials, and distribution challenges, providing insight into the specific areas where improvements can be made to boost efficiency and market reach.
- Chapter VI: Design of the Cloud-Based Supply Chain Model
  This chapter presents the proposed cloud-based information system model, detailing its components and functionality. It

describes the data flow between MSEs, suppliers, and distributors, and illustrates how the system can facilitate better inventory management, communication, and collaboration across the supply chain.
- Chapter VII: Summary and Future Applications
  The final chapter summarizes the key points covered in the monograph, discussing the expected impact of the proposed information system on the apple agro-industry. It also suggests possible applications for similar agro-industries and points out opportunities for further refinement and adaptation of the model in other agricultural sectors.

This structure aims to guide readers through the process of developing a practical, cloud-based solution for MSEs in the agro-industry, offering insights that are both relevant for business practitioners and useful for readers interested in supply chain innovation.

CHAPTER II: SUPPLY CHAIN MANAGEMENT IN THE AGRO-INDUSTRY

2.1 Definition and History of Supply Chain Management

Supply Chain Management (SCM) is the coordination and integration of all activities involved in the movement and transformation of goods, from raw materials to final products, including the management of information, resources, and finances along the entire process (Russell, 2007). SCM integrates multiple functions across a network of suppliers, manufacturers, distributors, and retailers to ensure that products reach end consumers efficiently and cost-effectively. This holistic approach goes beyond mere logistics; it involves enhancing the effectiveness of the flow of material, information and money (Sahin & Robinson, 2007).

The term "supply chain" was first conceptualized by Keith Oliver, a management consultant at Booz Allen Hamilton, in the early 1980s. Oliver's approach emphasized breaking down functional barriers between production, marketing, and distribution, promoting a seamless flow across departments to boost efficiency and responsiveness (Russell, 2007). This concept evolved as companies increasingly recognized the importance of collaborating with suppliers and distributors to create a cohesive network, rather than viewing each segment as isolated. By the mid-1980s, JB Houlihan expanded the SCM framework by emphasizing the relationship between shared information, coordinated decision-making, and mutual benefits across the supply chain (Russell, 2007).

Since then, supply chain management has grown to become a central focus for industries aiming to enhance competitive advantage in a globalized market. In the agro-industry, SCM addresses the unique needs of managing perishable goods, seasonal production cycles, and fluctuating demand. Agro-industrial supply chains are often complex and time-sensitive, as they deal with fresh produce that must be delivered promptly and preserved properly to retain quality. Effective SCM in this sector not only improves operational efficiency but also plays a critical role in minimizing waste, reducing costs, and meeting stringent quality standards (Afonso & Cabrita, 2015; Bourlakis et al., 2014).

The adoption of SCM in the agro-industry has also been influenced by rapid technological advancements. Information Technology (IT) is one main facilitator for excellence strategic Supply chain. Furthermore, the ability to share information and collaborative capabilities will affect the performance of the supply chain (Wu et al. 2014). For MSEs in the apple agro-industry, such as those in Batu City, integrating supply chain management practices can lead to significant improvements in cost efficiency, product quality, and customer satisfaction. These businesses can achieve better coordination, faster response times, and higher reliability by adopting SCM principles tailored to their specific needs.

Overall, SCM continues to evolve with innovations such as cloud computing, automation, and advanced analytics, further enabling the agro-industry to optimize every link in the supply chain. As the agro-industry adopts these advancements, MSEs can expect greater opportunities to overcome traditional limitations, scale their operations, and enhance their presence in both local and global markets.

2.2 Supply Chain Management in Horticulture

Supply Chain Management (SCM) in horticulture addresses the unique requirements and challenges of managing the flow of perishable agricultural goods from producers to consumers. Unlike other industries, the horticultural supply chain must consider the limited shelf life of products, seasonal production cycles, and variability in product quality, which depend on factors such as weather conditions and crop yield (Gokarn & Kuthambalayan, 2019) Effective SCM in horticulture is essential to maintaining the freshness and quality of products, minimizing waste, and meeting consumer demand.

In the horticultural sector, SCM involves coordinating multiple stages, including raw material sourcing, harvesting, processing, storage, transportation, and distribution (Indrajit & Djokopranoto, 2002). Each stage requires careful planning and management to ensure that products reach the end consumer in optimal condition. For example, the handling of apples in agro-industries, such as those in Batu City, East Java, involves ensuring that harvested apples are processed, stored, and transported in ways that preserve their quality, taste, and nutritional value. A robust SCM framework can also reduce post-harvest losses, which are often high in horticulture due to inadequate storage facilities and delayed transportation (Gardas et al., 2018).

One of the key components of SCM in horticulture is the integration of information technology, which helps manage the complexities of coordinating multiple actors across the supply chain (Montoya-Torres & Ortiz-Vargas, 2014). Technologies such as inventory management systems, demand forecasting tools, and automated ordering processes allow for better planning, real-time tracking, and efficient inventory turnover, which is crucial for perishable products. For instance, demand forecasting enables producers and suppliers to align production and distribution with market demand, thus reducing the risk of overproduction and waste (Reyes et al., 2023).

Collaboration between actors in the horticultural supply chain is also critical. Unlike more predictable industries, horticulture faces high levels of uncertainty in both production and demand. Effective SCM strategies in this sector focus on creating partnerships between producers, suppliers, processors, and distributors to improve information sharing, joint planning, and decision-making (Wu et al., 2014). Through collaborative practices, horticultural MSEs can adapt more effectively to fluctuations in supply and demand, manage risks, and implement quality control measures across the supply chain.

In recent years, sustainability has become a core focus in SCM for horticulture, as businesses seek to minimize their environmental footprint while enhancing operational efficiency (Agbelusi et al., 2024). For MSEs in the apple agro-industry, sustainable practices are increasingly relevant, as consumers show a preference for eco-friendly products and practices that support local agriculture.

Overall, SCM in horticulture is a dynamic and complex process that requires a tailored approach to manage the perishable nature of goods, fluctuating supply and demand, and the need for close collaboration among all participants. With advancements in technology and a growing emphasis on sustainability, horticultural supply chains are increasingly equipped to meet these challenges, allowing MSEs to improve product quality, reduce costs, and meet consumer expectations more effectively.

2.3 Key Success Factors in Supply Chain Management

The success of Supply Chain Management (SCM) in any industry, including horticulture, depends on several key factors that enhance operational efficiency, responsiveness, and competitiveness. For the horticultural sector, where MSEs face unique challenges such as product perishability, seasonal variability, and fluctuating market demand, these success factors are essential in establishing a robust and sustainable supply chain. The primary success factors in SCM are detailed as follows:

1. Efficient Information Sharing and Communication

   Effective SCM relies heavily on seamless information flow among all actors in the supply chain, from suppliers to retailers (Tutuhatunewa et al., 2019). For MSEs in the horticultural sector, having access to real-time data on inventory levels, market demand, and product availability helps coordinate activities and avoid disruptions. Studies highlight that information sharing improves decision-making and reduces uncertainty in supply chains (Wu et al., 2014). Cloud-based systems, for instance, facilitate real-time communication, ensuring that all stakeholders have up-to-date information on supply and demand dynamics.

2. Collaboration and Strategic Partnerships

   Building collaborative relationships between supply chain actors enhances trust, mutual support, and flexibility. In the horticultural supply chain, strategic partnerships with suppliers, distributors, and retailers help MSEs manage risks and respond quickly to changes in market conditions. Collaborative practices, such as joint planning and shared resources, are especially valuable in horticulture, where factors like harvest timing and product shelf life are critical. Through close collaboration, MSEs can achieve a more reliable and efficient supply chain (Montoya-Torres & Ortiz-Vargas, 2014).

3. Adoption of Advanced Technology

   Technological advancements play a significant role in optimizing supply chain performance (Dozier & Chang, 2007). Implementing technologies such as cloud computing, inventory management systems, and demand forecasting tools allows MSEs to streamline their operations, reduce costs, and increase scalability. In the horticultural industry, these tools help manage perishability by enabling better control over production, storage, and distribution.

4. Efficient Inventory and Transportation Management

   Efficient inventory and transportation management are essential for minimizing delays, reducing storage costs, and ensuring timely delivery of fresh products. Horticultural MSEs benefit from practices that reduce lead times and optimize logistics, such as selecting cost-effective transport routes and scheduling deliveries to maintain product quality. Transportation is a significant cost factor in SCM, especially in agriculture, where products are often produced in rural areas and consumed in urban markets (Sadegheih et al., 2010). Optimizing transport schedules and inventory turnover helps MSEs meet consumer demand promptly.

5. Focus on Quality and Sustainability

   Quality control and sustainability are increasingly important in modern SCM. Consumers today expect high-quality products that are produced responsibly. For horticultural MSEs, maintaining consistent product quality and adopting sustainable practices—such as reducing emissions in transportation, optimizing resource use, and minimizing waste—are vital for competitive advantage (Simpson et al., 2004). Sustainable SCM practices also align with consumer preferences for eco-friendly products, benefiting MSEs by enhancing brand reputation and customer loyalty.

6. Flexibility and Responsiveness to Market Changes

In the rapidly evolving agricultural market, supply chains must be adaptable to changes in consumer preferences, seasonal availability, and economic conditions. Flexibility enables MSEs to adjust production and distribution in response to market demand fluctuations. A flexible SCM approach, which includes maintaining alternative suppliers, adapting production schedules, and using agile logistics solutions, allows MSEs in horticulture to navigate uncertainties effectively (Wang & Yang, 2022). Skilled Workforce and Training

A skilled workforce equipped with SCM knowledge and technical expertise is essential for effectively managing supply chain operations. Training employees in areas like inventory management, logistics, and quality control helps improve efficiency and reduce errors. For MSEs, investing in workforce development also promotes adaptability, enabling employees to respond effectively to challenges and changes in the supply chain (Russell, 2007).

These key success factors provide a framework for MSEs in the horticultural supply chain to enhance their operations, manage risks, and build resilience. By prioritizing efficient information sharing, collaboration, technological adoption, and sustainable practices, MSEs can strengthen their position within the supply chain, achieving better market responsiveness and customer satisfaction.

Chapter III: Cloud Computing Technology

3.1 Overview of Cloud Computing

Cloud computing is a transformative technology that allows businesses to access computing resources—such as storage, processing power, and software—over the internet, rather than relying on local servers or physical hardware. This technology enables users to leverage high-powered computing infrastructure and services on a pay-as-you-go basis, making it accessible and scalable for businesses of all sizes, including Micro and Small Enterprises (MSEs) (Hutchinson et al., 2009). Cloud computing eliminates the need for costly investments in IT infrastructure, as users can access these resources remotely and scale their usage according to demand.

Cloud computing is characterized by its three primary service models: Software as a Service (SaaS), Platform as a Service (PaaS), and Infrastructure as a Service (IaaS). Each of these models offers distinct advantages and is suited to different aspects of business operations:

1. Software as a Service (SaaS): SaaS provides businesses with access to software applications hosted in the cloud, which users can operate via a web browser or app without installing or maintaining the software locally. Examples include customer relationship management (CRM) systems, office productivity tools, and specialized applications like inventory management systems. SaaS is beneficial for MSEs as it reduces the need for technical expertise and allows immediate access to updated applications (Singh et al., 2015).

2. Platform as a Service (PaaS): PaaS offers a cloud environment where users can develop, test, and deploy their applications without managing underlying infrastructure, such as servers and storage. This model is particularly useful for businesses that need to create customized applications, as

it provides a flexible and scalable environment with built-in development tools. PaaS is often used by businesses looking to integrate new features and services into their existing systems (Mahmood, 2011).

3. Infrastructure as a Service (IaaS): IaaS provides virtualized computing resources over the internet, such as servers, storage, and networks. It allows businesses to avoid investing in physical servers and related infrastructure, instead of renting resources on demand. This model provides maximum flexibility, enabling users to configure their own operating systems, storage solutions, and applications. IaaS is ideal for businesses requiring significant storage or custom setups that are cost-prohibitive on local servers (Mahmood, 2011)

The adoption of cloud computing offers several benefits that align with the needs of MSEs in the agro-industry. These include scalability, flexibility, and cost-efficiency, which allow small enterprises to operate with the same technological advantages as larger organizations. Cloud computing enhances operational agility, enabling businesses to adjust resources quickly in response to demand fluctuations, and supports data accessibility, as information stored in the cloud can be accessed from any location with an internet connection.

In addition to operational benefits, cloud computing can foster collaboration and integration within supply chains, as it supports real-time data sharing and communication among supply chain actors. This aspect is crucial for the apple agro-industry, where timely information sharing between suppliers, producers, and distributors helps improve supply chain efficiency and responsiveness (Sinha, 2013). By enabling MSEs to share inventory data, monitor supply levels, and coordinate deliveries, cloud-based systems strengthen the overall supply chain network.

As cloud computing continues to evolve, it incorporates advanced capabilities such as artificial intelligence (AI), machine learning (ML), and the Internet of Things (IoT), further expanding its potential in supply chain management. These advancements enable predictive analytics for demand forecasting, automated quality control, and real-time monitoring of production and logistics, empowering MSEs to make data-driven decisions and improve overall efficiency (Assante et al., 2016).

By embracing cloud technology, small businesses in the apple agro-industry can overcome traditional limitations in resources and technical capacity, positioning themselves more competitively in a digital economy.

3.2 Service Models: SaaS, PaaS, and IaaS

Cloud computing encompasses three primary service models, each designed to meet different technological needs: Software as a Service (SaaS), Platform as a Service (PaaS), and Infrastructure as a Service (IaaS). Each model provides distinct capabilities, allowing businesses, including Micro and Small Enterprises (MSEs), to choose the most suitable solution for their operations without requiring substantial investments in physical infrastructure. Below is an exploration of each model and its potential applications in the agro-industrial supply chain.

1. Software as a Service (SaaS)

Software as a Service (SaaS) allows businesses to access software applications over the internet, hosted by third-party providers, without the need for installation or maintenance on local devices. SaaS applications are typically accessed through web browsers, offering users flexibility and mobility. Examples include Google

Workspace, Microsoft Office 365, and specialized applications for supply chain management and inventory control.

For MSEs in the apple agro-industry, SaaS can provide essential tools for managing sales, inventory, customer relationships, and logistics. By leveraging SaaS solutions, businesses avoid the need for in-house IT expertise and infrastructure, as the service provider handles software maintenance, updates, and data security (Singh et al., 2015). SaaS tools for supply chain management can include functionalities such as:

- **Inventory Management**: Real-time tracking of stock levels, allowing MSEs to reduce waste and improve order fulfillment.
- **Order Processing**: Streamlined workflows for receiving, processing, and tracking customer orders, enhancing response times.
- **Customer Relationship Management (CRM)**: Tools for managing customer interactions and improving service quality.

With SaaS, MSEs can operate with the same technological advantages as larger businesses, gaining immediate access to high-quality applications that enhance productivity and coordination along the supply chain.

2. Platform as a Service (PaaS)

Platform as a Service (PaaS) provides a cloud-based environment where users can develop, test, and deploy their own applications without the need to manage underlying infrastructure, such as servers and storage. PaaS solutions offer a range of development tools, databases, and frameworks, making it easier and faster for developers to create customized applications suited to specific business needs. Examples of PaaS platforms include Google App Engine, Microsoft Azure, and Salesforce App Cloud.

In the context of the apple agro-industry, PaaS can be instrumental in developing custom applications tailored to the unique requirements of MSEs. For instance, an MSE could use PaaS to develop a mobile app for real-time coordination between apple suppliers, distributors, and retailers, enhancing supply chain visibility. PaaS benefits for MSEs in the agro-industry include:

- **Customization**: The ability to create applications specific to inventory, logistics, or quality control processes within the supply chain.
- **Scalability**: On-demand resource allocation to handle varying production or sales levels, especially during peak seasons.
- **Data Integration**: Enhanced data flow across different platforms, allowing seamless integration of supply chain information with CRM or ERP systems.

PaaS offers flexibility for MSEs that want to expand their digital capabilities without incurring the high costs of physical infrastructure or specialized IT staff. It is a powerful tool for innovation, enabling small businesses to tailor solutions that align with their operational workflows.

3. *Infrastructure as a Service (IaaS)*

Infrastructure as a Service (IaaS) provides businesses with virtualized computing resources, such as servers, storage, and networking, that are fully managed by the cloud provider. This model offers maximum control and flexibility, allowing users to configure their own operating systems, storage configurations, and applications. Notable examples of IaaS providers include Amazon Web Services (AWS), Microsoft Azure, and Google Cloud Platform.

For MSEs in the agro-industry, IaaS can support a more robust IT infrastructure without the need for investing in physical servers. This is particularly useful for businesses that require extensive storage for large volumes of data, such as supply chain records, customer orders, and product inventories. Key applications of IaaS in the supply chain context include:

- Data Storage and Backup: Secure, scalable storage solutions that support the storage of operational data, allowing for easy access, backup, and recovery.
- Computing Power for Data Analysis: High-performance computing capabilities that enable MSEs to run data-intensive applications, such as demand forecasting and inventory optimization.
- Disaster Recovery and Business Continuity: Reliable backup and recovery options to safeguard data and ensure uninterrupted operations in case of technical failures or data breaches.

IaaS is an ideal option for MSEs that need flexibility in managing their IT environments, especially if they are handling sensitive data or need to accommodate rapid growth. By using IaaS, small enterprises can scale resources up or down based on demand, ensuring cost-effectiveness while maintaining high operational standards.

Summary of Service Model Benefits

Each cloud computing service model—SaaS, PaaS, and IaaS—offers unique advantages, allowing MSEs in the apple agro-industry to select or combine models that best fit their requirements:

- SaaS provides ready-to-use applications for daily operations, supporting sales, customer management, and logistics.
- PaaS offers a flexible development platform for creating

custom applications tailored to specific supply chain needs.
- IaaS delivers foundational infrastructure resources, ideal for storage, data processing, and secure, scalable IT environments.

By leveraging these cloud service models, MSEs can improve collaboration, data accessibility, and responsiveness across their supply chains, enabling them to operate more competitively and efficiently in a challenging market environment (Assante et al., 2016; Mahmood, 2011; Singh et al., 2015).

CHAPTER IV: APPROACH TO DEVELOPING THE SUPPLY CHAIN MODEL

4.1 Approach and Methods

To develop a practical and effective cloud-based supply chain model for the apple agro-industry, a systematic approach was taken to understand the specific needs and challenges faced by Micro and Small Enterprises (MSEs) in this sector. The following approach and methods outline the steps and techniques used to collect, analyze, and apply data for constructing the proposed model.

1. Research Design

This study adopted a mixed-methods design, combining qualitative and quantitative approaches to gain comprehensive insights into the supply chain operations of MSEs in the apple agro-industry. The mixed-methods approach was chosen to allow for both in-depth exploration and statistical analysis, providing a richer understanding of the current supply chain landscape and the potential impact of cloud computing technology on MSE performance.

2. Data Collection Techniques

Two primary data collection methods were utilized:

- Surveys and Questionnaires: Structured surveys were administered to a sample of MSE owners, managers, and key supply chain personnel. The surveys included questions about current supply chain practices, challenges in inventory and logistics management, collaboration with suppliers and distributors, and awareness of cloud computing applications. The quantitative data collected from the surveys helped quantify the extent of these issues, providing a baseline for assessing potential improvements with cloud technology.
- Interviews and Focus Groups: In addition to surveys, semi-structured interviews and focus group discussions were

conducted with selected MSEs, suppliers, and distributors. This qualitative approach allowed for a deeper exploration of the operational challenges faced by these actors, especially in terms of data sharing, order coordination, and inventory control. Focus groups fostered collaborative discussions, encouraging participants to share their perspectives on cloud computing's potential benefits and their readiness to adopt new technologies.

3. Sampling Methods

Given the focus on the apple agro-industry in Batu City, East Java, a purposive sampling technique was used to select MSEs that are actively involved in apple processing and distribution. This non-probability sampling approach was chosen to ensure that the selected participants represent the typical characteristics of MSEs in the local agro-industry. Within this framework, convenience sampling was also applied to include participants who were accessible and willing to provide data on their supply chain practices.

4. Data Analysis Techniques

- Descriptive Analysis: The survey data was analyzed using descriptive statistics to summarize responses regarding supply chain challenges, inventory practices, and current technological adoption levels. This analysis provided an overview of the operational status of MSEs in the apple agro-industry and highlighted common issues such as stockouts, delivery delays, and coordination problems.
- Thematic Analysis: Qualitative data from interviews and focus groups were analyzed using thematic analysis to identify recurring themes and patterns in participants' responses. This approach helped categorize the core supply chain issues, such as the lack of real-time information, ineffective communication, and challenges in resource allocation. The insights derived from thematic analysis guided the design of the cloud-based model to address these

specific issues.

5. Development of the Cloud-Based Model

Based on the findings from data collection and analysis, a cloud-based supply chain model was developed. The model was designed to address key challenges identified in the study, including inventory control, data sharing, and supplier collaboration. The development process involved the following steps:

- Identifying Functional Requirements: The specific functions needed to improve supply chain operations—such as real-time inventory tracking, automated order processing, and data sharing—were identified from the survey and interview data. These functions were then mapped to appropriate cloud computing service models, such as SaaS for inventory management and PaaS for custom application development.
- System Design and Flow Mapping: The proposed model's design included a flow chart outlining the data flow among actors in the supply chain. This visualization demonstrated how information, inventory status, and order details would be shared among suppliers, MSEs, and distributors using cloud platforms. A combination of SaaS and PaaS layers was selected to provide a flexible and scalable solution tailored to the needs of the apple agro-industry.
- Validation through Expert Feedback: To ensure the feasibility and effectiveness of the model, feedback was solicited from industry experts and technology consultants familiar with cloud computing and SCM. Their input helped refine the model, particularly in selecting suitable cloud platforms and ensuring user-friendliness for MSEs with limited technical expertise.

6. Evaluation Metrics

To assess the model's effectiveness, several key performance indicators (KPIs) were defined, including inventory turnover rate, order fulfillment accuracy, lead time reduction, and overall supply chain responsiveness. These metrics were chosen to evaluate improvements in supply chain efficiency, customer satisfaction, and the operational performance of MSEs in the apple agro-industry.

The approach and methods employed in this study provided a structured framework for understanding the unique challenges faced by MSEs in the apple agro-industry. By combining quantitative data from surveys with qualitative insights from interviews, a comprehensive view of supply chain dynamics was established. This data-driven approach informed the design of a cloud-based model that offers practical solutions tailored to the needs of MSEs, fostering a more efficient, responsive, and technologically advanced supply chain.

4.2 Selecting Participants for Model Development

To create a comprehensive and relevant supply chain model for the apple agro-industry, participants were carefully chosen to represent the range of Micro and Small Enterprises (MSEs) involved in apple production, processing, and distribution in Batu City, East Java. By selecting businesses with varied roles in the supply chain, the approach aimed to gather diverse perspectives on operational challenges and opportunities for improvement. This section describes the process used to identify and engage participants in the model development process.

1. Targeted Selection of Key Supply Chain Actors

The main selection method focused on identifying key actors within the apple agro-industry who play critical roles in different stages of the supply chain. This targeted approach prioritized MSEs that could provide valuable insights based on their specific experiences and challenges in the apple supply chain. By focusing on businesses involved directly in apple sourcing, processing, and distribution, the approach captured essential viewpoints that would inform the design of a relevant and effective model.

Key participants included:

- Apple Growers and Raw Material Suppliers: Providing insights on harvesting cycles, quality control, and pricing challenges.
- Processing Enterprises: Including businesses that transform raw apples into products like chips, cider, and vinegar, helping to highlight production and inventory management needs.
- Distributors and Retailers: Offering perspectives on market demand, order processing, and delivery coordination, critical to understanding end-to-end supply chain dynamics.

2. Engagement of Accessible Participants

To streamline the process, businesses that were more accessible and open to sharing their experiences were given priority. This approach allowed the project to efficiently gather input from those MSEs most able to contribute, balancing the need for broad representation with practical considerations of time and availability. This method of engaging accessible participants was particularly helpful in gathering real-life examples of common supply chain challenges and data-sharing practices.

3. Diversity of Business Roles and Perspectives

The selection process included a variety of businesses across different stages of the apple agro-industry supply chain. By ensuring diversity in business roles, the approach aimed to reflect the entire supply chain ecosystem, encompassing sourcing, processing, and distribution functions. This diversity of participants provided a well-rounded view of the sector, offering insights that could be used to address both common and unique challenges in the supply chain.

Through this thoughtful selection process, the participants offered insights that contributed to developing a practical, cloud-based model designed to enhance efficiency, coordination, and responsiveness across the apple agro-industry supply chain. The input from these key stakeholders helped shape the model to meet the specific operational needs of MSEs in the sector.

4.3 Gathering and Understanding Data

To build a cloud-based supply chain model that accurately reflects the needs of Micro and Small Enterprises (MSEs) in the apple agro-industry, data was gathered through methods designed to capture real-world challenges and practices. This section explains the approach used to gather information from various actors in the supply chain, as well as the steps taken to interpret this information for model development.

1. Information Gathering from Supply Chain Participants

Data collection focused on understanding the daily operations, constraints, and requirements of MSEs involved in apple production, processing, and distribution. Information was gathered through:

- Conversations and Interviews: Engaging with business owners, managers, and staff in informal conversations and structured interviews provided firsthand insights into their challenges. Topics included current practices in inventory management, order processing, supplier coordination, and their familiarity with digital tools.
- Observations of Supply Chain Processes: Direct observations allowed a closer look at how MSEs manage supply chain tasks, from sourcing raw apples to fulfilling customer orders. This provided valuable context for understanding pain points like stock management, delays in delivery, and data entry

practices.
- Feedback on Technology Use: Participants were asked about their experiences with existing technology and potential barriers to adopting new digital solutions. This feedback highlighted the readiness of MSEs to adopt cloud-based tools and their specific needs for features like data sharing and order tracking.

2. *Examining Patterns and Key Themes*

The information gathered was analyzed to identify recurring themes and patterns in the supply chain practices of MSEs. The focus was on recognizing common challenges and opportunities for improvement, such as:
- Inventory and Stock Visibility: MSEs frequently expressed difficulties in keeping track of stock levels and planning orders effectively. Limited visibility into available stock and future demand patterns often led to stock out or excess inventory, affecting both costs and customer satisfaction.
- Communication Gaps in the Supply Chain: A recurring theme was the lack of real-time communication between suppliers, producers, and distributors. This gap often led to delays, miscommunication about order status, and missed opportunities for collaboration.
- Interest in Simple, Scalable Solutions: Many MSEs showed interest in digital solutions but expressed concerns about complexity and cost. These insights guided the design of a cloud-based model that would be user-friendly, affordable, and scalable for businesses of different sizes.

3. *Using Insights to Shape the Model*

The themes and patterns identified through data gathering formed the basis for developing a practical and responsive cloud-based supply chain model. This model was designed to address the specific challenges observed, including inventory management, communication, and ease of use. Key features prioritized in the model included:

- Real-Time Inventory Tracking: To address stock visibility challenges, the model incorporates tools for monitoring inventory levels in real time, helping MSEs make informed purchasing and production decisions.
- Centralized Communication Platform: To close communication gaps, the model provides a shared platform where suppliers, producers, and distributors can exchange information on order status, stock availability, and delivery schedules.
- User-Friendly Design: Based on feedback, the model emphasizes ease of use, enabling MSEs to access and utilize the tools without extensive training or additional costs.

Through this process of gathering and understanding data, the model was crafted to meet the real operational needs of the apple agro-industry, supporting MSEs in improving their supply chain efficiency, coordination, and responsiveness. The insights obtained from participants helped create a model that is both practical and adaptable to the dynamic nature of the agro-industry supply chain.

4.4 Scope and Considerations

While developing a cloud-based supply chain model for MSEs in the apple agro-industry, certain limitations and considerations impacted the data collection, analysis, and overall model design. Recognizing these limitations provides context to the model's applicability and highlights areas for future enhancement.

1. Geographical and Participant Scope

The model was developed based on insights gathered from MSEs operating in Batu City, East Java. This regional focus means that certain challenges, practices, or preferences may reflect specific local conditions and may not fully represent MSEs in other regions. Variability in market access, infrastructure, and technological readiness across different areas could influence the model's effectiveness if applied more broadly.

2. Sample Size and Representation

Given time and resource constraints, a select number of MSEs, suppliers, and distributors were engaged. While these participants provided valuable insights, a larger sample could have added depth and allowed for a more comprehensive understanding of the apple agro-industry supply chain. Consequently, the model may need adjustments to accommodate other business practices or challenges not captured in this initial group (Montoya-Torres & Ortiz-Vargas, 2014).

3. Dependence on Self-Reported Data

Many of the insights relied on self-reported data from surveys and interviews. While efforts were made to ensure accuracy, self-reporting can introduce biases, such as overestimating or underestimating specific challenges or the readiness to adopt technology. Observational methods helped counterbalance this limitation but may still reflect subjective perspectives of participants (Cook et al., 2011).

4. Technological Adoption and Readiness

The model assumes that MSEs possess a basic level of readiness for adopting cloud-based tools. However, technological adoption levels vary widely, with some businesses potentially lacking the infrastructure or skills needed to utilize cloud computing effectively. This variability could limit the immediate applicability of the model for some MSEs, requiring a phased approach or additional support to facilitate technology adoption.

5. Evolving Market and Environmental Conditions

Supply chains in the agro-industry are subject to changes in market demand, seasonal cycles, and environmental factors that impact production and distribution. While the model was designed to be flexible and adaptable, external factors like fluctuating apple yields or sudden changes in demand can influence its effectiveness, requiring ongoing adjustments and updates.

CHAPTER V: INSIGHTS INTO THE APPLE AGRO-INDUSTRY SUPPLY CHAIN

5.1 Characteristics of MSEs in the Apple Agro-Industry

Micro and Small Enterprises (MSEs) in the apple agro-industry play a crucial role in transforming raw apples into diverse value-added products, contributing to local economies and employment. These businesses typically handle various stages of the apple supply chain, including sourcing, processing, and distributing products such as apple cider, vinegar, chips, and other apple-based goods. Understanding the unique characteristics of these MSEs provides insight into the operational challenges they face and highlights areas where technological improvements, like cloud computing, can make a substantial difference.

1. Diverse Product Offerings

MSEs in the apple agro-industry commonly engage in product diversification to maximize the economic value of apples. The range of products includes fresh apple cider, dehydrated apple chips, apple vinegar, and other processed items. This diversification not only enhances income potential but also enables MSEs to adapt to changing market demands. However, managing multiple product lines adds complexity to inventory control, production planning, and quality assurance, often requiring specific strategies for handling raw materials and finished goods.

2. Seasonal and Perishable Nature of Raw Materials

The apple agro-industry is highly seasonal, with raw apple availability peaking during harvest seasons. The perishable nature of apples imposes additional pressures on MSEs to process or sell products quickly, as delayed handling can lead to spoilage and financial loss. This seasonality requires MSEs to plan operations around harvest cycles, manage variable supply levels, and implement efficient storage and processing practices to maintain product quality throughout the year.

3. Resource Constraints and Limited Economies of Scale

MSEs in this sector often operate with limited resources, including financial capital, skilled labor, and advanced technology. These constraints affect their ability to scale production, access broader markets, and invest in efficiency-enhancing technologies. Small-scale operations typically do not benefit from economies of scale, which can lead to higher per-unit costs in procurement, production, and distribution. This constraint further emphasizes the need for scalable, cost-effective technological solutions, such as cloud-based systems, to help optimize their operations within limited budgets.

4. Reliance on Conventional Markets and Distribution Channels

Most MSEs in the apple agro-industry rely on local markets and traditional distribution networks, such as direct sales to local stores, markets, or consignment-based arrangements with retailers. This limited market reach restricts growth opportunities and can lead to intense competition among local producers. Additionally, dependence on conventional markets means that many MSEs face challenges in reaching a wider customer base, which limits their ability to increase sales volumes and establish stronger market presence.

5. Challenges in Supply Chain Coordination and Communication

Coordination with suppliers, distributors, and retailers is a recurring challenge for MSEs. Given the typical lack of real-time data-sharing mechanisms, communication across the supply chain often involves manual or delayed processes, such as phone calls or in-person meetings. These manual practices contribute to inefficiencies, including inventory mismatches, delays in order processing, and frequent miscommunications regarding supply and demand. Effective supply chain coordination is further hindered by the limited use of technology, making it difficult for MSEs to achieve responsive and agile supply chain operations.

6. Low Adoption of Digital and Cloud-Based Tools

Despite the growing availability of digital tools, the adoption of advanced technologies remains low among MSEs in the apple agro-industry. Many businesses continue to rely on manual processes for managing inventory, recording sales, and coordinating with suppliers. The primary reasons for this low adoption include limited financial resources, lack of technical knowledge, and concerns about the complexity of implementing digital systems. As a result, operational inefficiencies persist, affecting the overall productivity and competitiveness of these enterprises.

7. Adaptability and Innovation in Response to Market Needs

One positive characteristic of MSEs in this industry is their adaptability and willingness to innovate in response to changing consumer preferences and market trends. Many MSEs demonstrate flexibility in their product offerings, adjusting recipes, packaging, and branding to cater to specific market segments. This adaptability is a valuable asset that allows these businesses to respond quickly to emerging demands. However, limited resources can constrain their ability to fully capitalize on these opportunities.

5.2 Supplier and Distributor Relations

Supplier and distributor relationships are crucial for the smooth functioning of the apple agro-industry supply chain. In the context of Micro and Small Enterprises (MSEs), these relationships significantly impact inventory management, production planning, and the ability to meet consumer demand. Understanding the dynamics between MSEs, suppliers, and distributors is essential for identifying areas where a cloud-based model can enhance communication, coordination, and efficiency across the supply chain.

1. Dependence on Local Suppliers for Raw Materials

MSEs in the apple agro-industry primarily rely on local suppliers for raw materials. These suppliers include apple farmers and other providers of essential inputs like food additives, packaging materials, and processing aids. Local suppliers often have limited production capacities and may be subject to seasonal variations in output, which directly affects the availability and cost of raw apples and other materials.

This dependency on local suppliers results in several challenges:
- Inconsistent Supply Levels: Seasonal production and supply fluctuations can lead to inconsistent availability of apples, impacting MSEs' ability to maintain steady production and meet market demand.
- Price Variability: Supply variations also lead to price fluctuations, which affect MSEs' cost structure and profitability.
- Limited Supplier Diversification: Due to local sourcing practices, MSEs often have few supplier options, which limits their ability to negotiate favorable terms or secure consistent quality.

2. Procurement and Payment Practices

The procurement process between MSEs and suppliers is often informal, with transactions commonly based on cash or consignment arrangements. Many MSEs make bulk purchases during the apple harvest season to take advantage of lower prices and higher availability, but this can strain cash flow and require significant upfront capital. Additionally, the lack of formal contracts or agreements with suppliers means that MSEs face risks related to supply consistency and quality.

The typical payment practices observed include:

- Cash Payments: Cash transactions are the most common payment method, particularly for smaller purchases. However, these payments can limit the purchasing power of MSEs during peak seasons.
- Consignment Arrangements: Some MSEs rely on consignment-based purchasing with delayed payments, allowing them to manage cash flow better. However, this arrangement can delay the procurement process, affecting timely production.

3. Coordination with Distributors and Retailers

Distributors and retailers play a vital role in connecting MSEs to the market. However, many MSEs rely on traditional distribution channels, such as local markets, small shops, and direct sales to consumers. This reliance limits market reach and often results in intense competition within the local area.

Key challenges in coordinating with distributors and retailers include:

- Manual Order Processing: Orders from distributors and retailers are often processed manually, leading to delays, errors, and inefficiencies. Without real-time order tracking, MSEs may face difficulties in managing inventory and fulfilling orders promptly.
- Limited Access to Broader Markets: MSEs typically have limited resources to expand their distribution network, restricting their ability to reach larger or more diverse consumer bases.

- Dependency on Retail Relationships: Many MSEs depend heavily on established relationships with retailers to sell their products. While these relationships can offer stability, they also limit MSEs' flexibility to explore new markets or negotiate better terms.

4. Communication Challenges

Communication across the supply chain—particularly with suppliers and distributors—remains a significant challenge for MSEs in the apple agro-industry. Given the low adoption of digital communication tools, most information is exchanged through phone calls or in-person meetings, which can be time-consuming and prone to misunderstandings. The lack of streamlined communication channels hampers coordination and responsiveness, leading to missed opportunities and operational inefficiencies.

Challenges in communication include:

- Delayed Information Exchange: Without a centralized platform for real-time data sharing, information about order status, inventory levels, and production schedules is often delayed, leading to disruptions in supply and demand alignment.
- Limited Transparency: Manual communication methods make it difficult to achieve full transparency between MSEs, suppliers, and distributors, which can create uncertainty about order fulfillment and stock availability.

5. *Opportunities for Improvement with Cloud-Based Solutions*

A cloud-based supply chain model presents significant opportunities to address the challenges in supplier and distributor relations. By adopting cloud technology, MSEs in the apple agro-industry can improve their communication, coordination, and data-sharing capabilities, enabling smoother relationships with suppliers and distributors. Key areas where cloud computing can enhance these relationships include:

- Real-Time Inventory and Order Tracking: A cloud-based system would allow suppliers, MSEs, and distributors to access real-time information on stock levels, order statuses, and delivery schedules. This visibility improves inventory management, minimizes delays, and helps all parties coordinate more effectively.
- Automated Ordering and Payment Processes: Automation tools can streamline order processing and payment methods, reducing the dependency on manual methods and mitigating cash flow constraints. Automated payment solutions can also facilitate smoother transactions between MSEs and suppliers, improving procurement efficiency.
- Enhanced Market Reach and Distribution Network: With a cloud-based system, MSEs can potentially expand their market reach by connecting with new distributors and retailers beyond their traditional networks. Digital communication and order management tools enable MSEs to scale their distribution network, explore new sales channels, and respond to broader market demands.
- Centralized Communication Platform: By implementing a centralized communication platform, cloud-based systems allow for faster, clearer, and more transparent communication among all supply chain actors. This platform reduces miscommunication, shortens response times, and fosters better relationships among suppliers, producers, and distributors.

5.3 Challenges in the Apple Agro-Industry Supply Chain

The apple agro-industry supply chain presents numerous challenges, particularly for Micro and Small Enterprises (MSEs) engaged in the production, processing, and distribution of apple-based products. These challenges stem from factors such as limited resources, market constraints, and coordination difficulties with suppliers and distributors. Addressing these challenges is essential for enhancing the efficiency and competitiveness of MSEs within the industry. This section outlines the main challenges faced by MSEs in the apple agro-industry supply chain.

1. Resource Constraints and Limited Scale

MSEs in the apple agro-industry often operate with limited financial and technical resources, which impacts their capacity to scale operations effectively. This limited scale prevents them from achieving economies of scale in production and procurement, resulting in higher per-unit costs for both raw materials and finished products (Simpson et al., 2004). Furthermore, limited access to financing can make it difficult for MSEs to invest in necessary equipment, technology, and infrastructure, which hampers productivity and restricts growth.

Resource constraints also influence other aspects of the supply chain:

- Production Capacity: Insufficient resources restrict the ability of MSEs to maintain consistent production volumes, especially during peak demand periods.
- Inventory Management: Limited financial resources often result in inefficient inventory practices, leading to either overstock or stockouts, both of which incur additional costs.
- Technological Adoption: With constrained budgets, MSEs have limited access to advanced technologies, including digital tools and cloud-based solutions that could optimize

supply chain processes.

2. Complexities in Supplier Relations

The apple agro-industry supply chain relies heavily on effective supplier relationships, yet MSEs frequently face challenges in managing these connections. Supplier relations are often informal and based on local networks, leading to issues such as inconsistent supply levels, fluctuating raw material quality, and variable pricing (Smith et al., 2007). Additionally, the seasonality of apple production further complicates these relationships, as raw material availability and quality vary depending on the harvest season.

Common issues in supplier relations include:

- Inconsistent Quality and Availability of Raw Materials: Seasonal production and limited access to diversified suppliers lead to fluctuations in apple quality and availability, making it challenging for MSEs to plan production consistently.
- Price Volatility: Changes in apple supply directly affect prices, creating uncertainty in cost management for MSEs, which are often unable to negotiate favorable terms due to their smaller scale.
- Dependency on Limited Suppliers: Many MSEs rely on a few local suppliers, which limits their bargaining power and increases vulnerability to supply chain disruptions, such as poor harvests or price hikes.

3. Market Access and Distribution Constraints

MSEs in the apple agro-industry commonly face barriers to expanding their market reach beyond local or regional markets. This limited market access constrains growth opportunities and often leads to intense competition within the local area. Traditional distribution networks, such as small shops and local markets, restrict MSEs' ability to reach a broader consumer base or establish a significant presence in larger retail markets (Moy & Luk, 2003).

Challenges related to market access and distribution include:

- Limited Reach to Broader Markets: Many MSEs rely on direct sales or consignment arrangements with local retailers, which limits their exposure to larger or geographically diverse markets.
- High Competition in Local Markets: As many MSEs are confined to selling in the same local markets, they face stiff competition, which puts downward pressure on prices and profitability.
- Restricted Resources for Marketing and Promotion: MSEs often lack the funds or expertise to invest in marketing strategies that could help them expand into new markets or create brand recognition, reducing their potential to attract a wider customer base.

4. Manual and Inefficient Processes

The reliance on manual processes in inventory tracking, order processing, and communication with suppliers and distributors leads to significant inefficiencies in the apple agro-industry supply chain. Many MSEs still rely on traditional methods, such as paper records and phone calls, for managing supply chain operations. This lack of automation contributes to delays, errors, and difficulties in scaling up operations.

Manual processes create challenges such as:

- Time-Consuming Data Entry and Record Keeping: Without digital systems, tracking inventory, sales, and orders requires significant manual effort, which is prone to error and difficult to scale.
- Communication Delays: Manual methods of communication, such as phone calls or in-person visits, slow down the coordination process, leading to inefficiencies in order

fulfillment and inventory management.
- Limited Data for Decision-Making: The absence of digital data management makes it challenging for MSEs to generate insights into inventory trends, demand forecasting, and supply chain performance, resulting in reactive rather than proactive management.

5. Coordination and Transparency Across the Supply Chain

Effective coordination and information sharing are essential for smooth supply chain operations, yet many MSEs in the apple agro-industry struggle with fragmented communication and limited transparency. Given the lack of centralized platforms for data sharing, information about inventory levels, order status, and production schedules is often fragmented or delayed. This results in misunderstandings, missed opportunities, and an inability to respond quickly to demand changes (Smith et al., 2007).

Coordination challenges include:

- Delayed Information Flow: Without a central platform, suppliers, MSEs, and distributors often operate with outdated information, resulting in supply chain bottlenecks and delays.
- Lack of Real-Time Visibility: Limited access to real-time inventory and order data reduces supply chain transparency, making it difficult for MSEs to align production with demand and inventory needs.
- Inadequate Response to Demand Changes: The inability to quickly adjust to fluctuations in demand or supply levels often leads to either shortages or excess inventory, both of which negatively impact profitability and customer satisfaction.

6. Limited Technological Adoption

While cloud-based and digital technologies could greatly enhance supply chain efficiency, their adoption remains low among MSEs in the apple agro-industry. Limited awareness, financial constraints, and a perceived complexity of technology contribute to this low adoption. As a result, many MSEs miss out on the potential advantages that technology could provide, such as real-time inventory tracking, automated ordering, and improved data analytics for decision-making (Simpson et al., 2004).

This low adoption of technology presents challenges such as:

- Operational Inefficiencies: Without digital tools, processes remain manual and inefficient, hindering productivity and scalability.
- Limited Competitive Advantage: In a market where competitors may adopt advanced technologies, MSEs that rely on traditional methods may find it increasingly challenging to keep pace.
- Missed Opportunities for Market Expansion: Digital tools can open doors to e-commerce platforms and broader distribution channels, which are not accessible to MSEs that have not embraced technological solutions.

CHAPTER VI: DEVELOPMENT OF A CLOUD-BASED SUPPLY CHAIN MODEL

6.1 Model Overview and Components

The proposed cloud-based supply chain model aims to address the unique needs and challenges faced by Micro and Small Enterprises (MSEs) in the apple agro-industry. By leveraging cloud computing technology, the model provides a centralized, scalable, and cost-effective solution that enhances inventory visibility, streamlines communication, and supports real-time decision-making. This section offers an overview of the model and its core components, each tailored to support different aspects of supply chain management.

Model Overview

The cloud-based supply chain model is designed to connect all key actors in the apple agro-industry supply chain, including suppliers, MSEs, and distributors, through a shared online platform. This model facilitates real-time data sharing and collaborative workflows, allowing each participant to access essential information about inventory levels, order status, production schedules, and market demand. The goal is to create a more transparent and responsive supply chain that empowers MSEs to optimize their operations and improve customer satisfaction.

The model operates on a layered architecture that integrates various cloud service models—Software as a Service (SaaS), Platform as a Service (PaaS), and Infrastructure as a Service (IaaS)—to provide comprehensive support for different functions within the supply chain. SaaS applications enable inventory and order management, PaaS facilitates customized app development, and IaaS offers secure, scalable storage for large volumes of data.

Key Components of the Model

1. Inventory Management System (SaaS)

   The inventory management system is a central component of the model, providing MSEs with real-time tracking of raw materials and finished products. This system automates stock updates and offers insights into current inventory levels, helping MSEs avoid overstocking or stockouts. Key features include:
   - Real-Time Stock Monitoring: Automated tracking of inventory levels with alerts for low stock, preventing production delays and optimizing replenishment cycles.
   - Expiration Date Tracking: Particularly useful for perishable products, this feature helps MSEs manage the freshness of their inventory, reducing waste and ensuring product quality.
   - Demand Forecasting Integration: Using historical sales data, the system provides demand forecasts to help MSEs plan inventory purchases in line with expected demand.

2. Order Processing and Tracking Module (SaaS)

   This module streamlines order management by automating order processing and tracking, reducing manual data entry and the potential for errors. It enables MSEs to manage incoming orders from distributors and retailers and provides real-time updates on order status. Features of this module include:
   - Automated Order Entry: Reduces the time and effort required for manual order processing, ensuring accuracy and consistency.
   - Order Status Tracking: Real-time updates allow all supply chain actors to view the current status of orders, from order placement to fulfillment.

- Customer Relationship Management (CRM) Integration: Links order data with customer information, helping MSEs manage customer interactions, preferences, and history, enhancing customer satisfaction.

3. Supplier and Distributor Communication Hub (PaaS)

    The communication hub is designed to facilitate seamless interaction between MSEs, suppliers, and distributors. Built on a Platform as a Service (PaaS) model, this component allows for real-time messaging, document sharing, and notifications across the supply chain. It fosters transparency, coordination, and quick responses to changes in supply or demand. Key features include:
    - Messaging and Notifications: Real-time messaging and automated notifications alert users to important updates, such as changes in order status, delivery schedules, or stock levels.
    - Shared Document Repository: Allows users to upload and access essential documents, including purchase orders, invoices, and shipping schedules, from a centralized location.
    - Collaborative Planning: Enables supply chain actors to coordinate on production schedules, inventory replenishment, and distribution plans, minimizing delays and miscommunications.

4. Data Analytics and Reporting Tool (PaaS)

    This tool provides MSEs with valuable insights into their supply chain performance through customizable reports and dashboards. The analytics tool helps businesses track key performance indicators (KPIs) related to inventory turnover, order fulfillment rates, and customer satisfaction. Core features include:
    - Customizable Dashboards: Visualize supply chain

data in easy-to-read charts and graphs, allowing MSEs to monitor KPIs at a glance.
- Predictive Analytics: Uses historical data to forecast demand trends, optimize inventory levels, and anticipate supply chain bottlenecks.
- Performance Reports: Generates reports on supplier performance, order accuracy, and delivery times, enabling continuous improvement and informed decision-making.

5. Scalable Storage and Data Security (IaaS)

The model relies on an Infrastructure as a Service (IaaS) layer for secure, scalable storage of large data volumes. This component supports the entire system, providing MSEs with a reliable platform to store inventory data, order histories, customer information, and other critical records. IaaS ensures data security and accessibility, even during peak usage periods. Key features include:
- Data Backup and Recovery: Automated backups ensure that data is protected and recoverable in case of system failures or cyber-attacks.
- Scalable Storage Capacity: Storage space can be increased or decreased based on demand, allowing MSEs to handle seasonal fluctuations without incurring unnecessary costs.
- Enhanced Security Protocols: Data encryption and access controls protect sensitive information, ensuring that only authorized users can access specific data.

6. Mobile Accessibility and User Interface

To make the model accessible and user-friendly for MSEs, a mobile-optimized interface is included. This feature allows supply chain actors to access key functions from smartphones or tablets, promoting flexibility and mobility for users who may need to manage operations on the go. Features include:

- Responsive Design: The interface adapts to different screen sizes, ensuring a seamless experience across devices.
- Easy Navigation: Intuitive menus and icons make it easy for users to access essential functions without extensive training.
- Offline Access: Limited offline functionality enables users to view important information, such as inventory levels and order statuses, even in areas with intermittent internet access.

6.2 Information Flow and Practical Applications

The cloud-based supply chain model for the apple agro-industry is designed to streamline the flow of information between suppliers, MSEs, and distributors, ensuring that essential data—such as inventory levels, order statuses, and production schedules—is accessible and up-to-date. This section illustrates how information flows within the model and provides practical examples of its use across different stages of the supply chain.

Information Flow in the Supply Chain Model

The model operates with centralized data storage and real-time information sharing to connect all actors in the supply chain. Key points in the information flow include:

1. Suppliers to MSEs: Suppliers enter data related to raw material availability, pricing, and quality specifications. This information is accessible in real time to MSEs, enabling them to make timely procurement decisions, maintain stock levels, and plan production efficiently.
2. MSEs to Distributors and Retailers: MSEs update information on available products, including stock levels, pricing, and expected delivery dates. Distributors and

retailers can access this data to check stock availability, place orders, and coordinate deliveries seamlessly.
3. Shared Communication and Coordination: Through a central communication hub, suppliers, MSEs, and distributors can exchange real-time updates, share documentation, and collaborate on production and distribution plans. Notifications alert relevant parties to any changes in inventory, orders, or delivery schedules, reducing the potential for misunderstandings and delays.
4. Data Analytics Feedback Loop: Data from inventory, orders, and customer interactions are analyzed to provide insights into supply chain performance, demand trends, and operational efficiencies. These insights help MSEs make informed adjustments to production schedules, reorder quantities, and improve coordination with supply chain partners.

Practical Applications of the Model

To illustrate the benefits of this cloud-based model, the following examples show how different components can be applied in real-world scenarios across the supply chain.

1. Optimizing Inventory Management

Scenario: An MSE producing apple vinegar experiences high demand during certain seasons and needs a reliable inventory system to ensure timely raw material sourcing and stock management.

Application: Using the inventory management system, the MSE tracks real-time stock levels and receives alerts when apple supplies are low. By checking supplier availability in the shared platform, the MSE can promptly reorder and maintain an adequate supply, reducing production delays and avoiding overstock.

2. Automating Order Processing

Scenario: A distributor places regular orders for apple chips to stock retail locations but has experienced delays in previous orders due to manual processing.

Application: The MSE can automate order entry through the order processing module. The distributor places the order directly within the platform, which automatically updates stock levels and notifies the production team. The system provides real-time order status, allowing the distributor to track the order from placement to delivery without manual follow-up.

3. Enhancing Supplier Coordination

Scenario: Due to an unexpected surge in demand, an MSE needs additional apples on short notice to meet production needs.

Application: Through the communication hub, the MSE can quickly contact suppliers to check for apple availability and negotiate expedited delivery. Suppliers update the MSE in real time, allowing for rapid decision-making. This flexibility minimizes disruptions and supports timely response to market demands.

4. Using Demand Forecasting to Plan Production

Scenario: Based on past sales data, an MSE producing apple cider anticipates higher demand in the upcoming holiday season and wants to adjust production accordingly.

Application: With data analytics tools integrated into the model, the MSE accesses demand forecasts based on historical sales and market trends. Using this forecast, the MSE plans production, adjusts raw material orders, and optimizes workforce allocation to meet expected demand, reducing last-minute adjustments and enhancing customer satisfaction.

5. Monitoring Supply Chain Performance and Making Adjustments

Scenario: The MSE wants to evaluate supplier performance to decide if they should explore additional supplier options for price and quality consistency.

Application: Using the model's performance analytics, the MSE reviews reports on each supplier's delivery times, product quality, and price variations over time. This data helps the MSE make informed decisions on supplier selection and negotiate better terms or consider diversification to improve supply chain resilience.

6.3 Benefits and Challenges of Implementing Cloud Solutions

The implementation of a cloud-based supply chain model for the apple agro-industry brings numerous benefits to Micro and Small Enterprises (MSEs), enabling them to operate more efficiently, improve data transparency, and enhance overall responsiveness to market demands. However, cloud adoption also presents specific challenges, particularly for smaller businesses that may face limitations in resources, technological readiness, and infrastructure. This section outlines the primary benefits and potential challenges of implementing cloud computing solutions in the supply chain.

Benefits of Cloud Implementation
1. Enhanced Data Flow and Real-Time Information Access
   One of the most significant advantages of a cloud-based supply chain model is the improvement in data flow across the supply chain. Cloud computing enables real-time sharing of inventory levels, order statuses, and production schedules,

allowing all actors—including suppliers, MSEs, and distributors—to access up-to-date information. This transparency reduces delays, prevents stockouts, and ensures that all participants can make timely decisions based on accurate data (Wu et al., 2014).
- Example: An MSE can instantly view stock levels and place orders based on supplier availability, while distributors can track order fulfillment status in real time, reducing the need for follow-up communication and enhancing coordination across the supply chain.

2. Scalability and Flexibility

Cloud-based solutions offer scalability that allows MSEs to adjust their data storage and processing needs based on seasonal fluctuations or business growth. This flexibility is particularly valuable for agro-industry MSEs, where demand and supply levels can vary significantly depending on harvest cycles and market trends (Yang et al., 2008). Cloud models can scale up during peak seasons and scale down during off-peak periods, ensuring cost-effectiveness and operational efficiency.
- Example: During peak harvest times, an MSE can increase storage capacity temporarily to manage a higher volume of inventory data without the need for permanent infrastructure expansion.

3. Cost Reduction and Resource Optimization

Cloud implementation reduces the need for on-premises infrastructure, minimizing upfront capital expenditures and lowering operational costs. Instead of investing in physical servers and dedicated IT resources, MSEs can pay for cloud services on a subscription or pay-as-you-go basis. This model allows smaller businesses to access advanced technology without a significant financial burden, thus optimizing resources and improving profitability (Sadegheih et al.,

2010).
- Example: MSEs can leverage cloud storage and processing power without large investments in hardware, allowing them to allocate their limited capital toward other business-critical activities, such as product development and marketing.

4. Improved Decision-Making through Data Analytics

Cloud-based analytics tools provide MSEs with insights into inventory trends, demand forecasts, and supplier performance, supporting data-driven decision-making. By analyzing data patterns, MSEs can optimize inventory levels, adjust production schedules, and improve customer service. Predictive analytics also enables proactive planning, allowing MSEs to anticipate and prepare for market changes (Wu et al., 2014).
- Example: An MSE can use demand forecasts generated by cloud-based analytics to adjust production during holiday seasons, reducing waste from overproduction and improving the likelihood of meeting customer demand.

5. Enhanced Collaboration and Communication

Cloud platforms provide a centralized space for communication, where supply chain actors can collaborate, share updates, and resolve issues efficiently. This enhanced communication promotes better coordination between suppliers, MSEs, and distributors, reducing miscommunications and facilitating a smoother workflow. With all participants accessing the same platform, everyone is aligned with the latest information (Yang et al., 2008).
- Example: Suppliers can inform MSEs of any delays in raw material availability immediately, allowing MSEs to adjust production schedules accordingly and minimize disruptions.

Challenges of Cloud Implementation

1. Limited Technological Readiness and Digital Literacy
   Many MSEs, especially those in traditional sectors like the agro-industry, may have limited experience with digital tools and cloud technology. The lack of technical knowledge and digital literacy can pose a barrier to successful cloud implementation, as employees may require training to use new systems effectively. Without adequate preparation, MSEs may face challenges in fully utilizing the model's capabilities (Wu et al., 2014).
   - Example: MSE employees may need guidance on using cloud-based inventory systems and communicating through digital platforms. Training efforts are essential to ensure smooth adoption and effective usage.

2. Dependence on Reliable Internet Connectivity
   Cloud-based solutions rely on stable internet connectivity, which can be challenging in rural or less-developed areas. Intermittent or slow internet access may disrupt data sharing and delay updates, undermining the model's effectiveness. In areas with unreliable internet, MSEs may experience reduced efficiency and fail to fully benefit from real-time cloud features (Sadegheih et al., 2010).
   - Example: An MSE located in a rural area may struggle with slow connectivity, making it difficult to access real-time data and coordinate with suppliers or distributors effectively.

3. Concerns Over Data Security and Privacy
   Data security is a significant concern for businesses implementing cloud solutions, especially for those handling sensitive information related to suppliers, customers, and production. MSEs may have reservations about storing data in the cloud due to fears of data breaches or unauthorized

access. Choosing a reputable cloud provider with strong security measures is essential to alleviate these concerns (Yang et al., 2008).
- Example: An MSE may worry about protecting financial data and customer information from unauthorized access or potential cyber-attacks, requiring them to ensure that their cloud provider offers robust security features, such as encryption and user authentication.

4. Initial Setup and Transition Costs

Although cloud solutions reduce long-term operational costs, MSEs may still face initial setup and transition expenses. These costs include system customization, data migration, and employee training. For small businesses with tight budgets, these initial costs may be a deterrent, even if the cloud model offers financial benefits over time (Wu et al., 2014).
- Example: An MSE may need to invest in training employees and customizing the cloud system to fit its unique operational needs, which requires an upfront investment despite the potential for long-term savings.

5. Resistance to Change and Cultural Adaptation

   Shifting from traditional methods to cloud-based solutions may encounter resistance among MSEs accustomed to manual or conventional practices. Change management is essential to help these businesses recognize the benefits of digital transformation and support a smooth transition. Without addressing this resistance, MSEs may struggle to adopt and effectively utilize the new system.
   - Example: Long-standing MSEs with entrenched manual processes may initially be hesitant to adopt cloud-based solutions. Clear communication of the benefits and gradual adaptation strategies can help ease the transition.

Chapter VII: Final Insights and Future Opportunities

7.1 Key Takeaways

This monograph explored the development and potential impact of a cloud-based supply chain model tailored for Micro and Small Enterprises (MSEs) in the apple agro-industry. The model was designed to address unique challenges in inventory management, supplier coordination, and market access, with the ultimate goal of enhancing the efficiency, responsiveness, and competitiveness of MSEs. Below are the key takeaways from the study:

1. Understanding the Apple Agro-Industry Supply Chain Needs
   The apple agro-industry supply chain is characterized by unique challenges, including seasonal variability, limited access to broader markets, and reliance on local suppliers. MSEs in this industry often face resource constraints and operate on small scales, which limits their ability to leverage economies of scale or invest in advanced technology. These factors collectively hinder their ability to maintain steady production, optimize inventory, and expand market reach. By identifying these needs, this work highlighted the critical role of digital solutions in addressing these barriers.
2. Benefits of a Cloud-Based Model for MSEs
   The cloud-based model offers a variety of benefits to MSEs in the apple agro-industry:
   - Real-Time Data Flow: The model facilitates seamless, real-time data sharing between suppliers, MSEs, and distributors, enabling MSEs to make timely and informed decisions regarding inventory levels, order fulfillment, and production schedules.
   - Enhanced Collaboration: A centralized communication platform fosters better coordination,

reducing the risk of miscommunication, delays, and order errors across the supply chain.
- o Scalability and Flexibility: Cloud solutions allow MSEs to scale resources up or down depending on seasonal demands, providing cost-effective storage, data processing, and access to essential tools that support growth.
- o Data-Driven Decision-Making: Through data analytics, MSEs gain insights into demand patterns, inventory trends, and supply chain performance, allowing them to anticipate needs and improve resource allocation.

3. Challenges in Cloud Implementation

While cloud computing brings numerous advantages, there are also challenges to consider:
- o Technological Readiness and Digital Literacy: Many MSEs lack experience with digital tools, requiring training and support to effectively adopt and leverage the cloud-based model.
- o Internet Reliability: Access to stable internet connectivity is crucial for cloud-based systems, but this can be a limiting factor for MSEs in rural or remote areas.
- o Data Security Concerns: MSEs must choose reliable cloud providers with strong security measures to protect sensitive supply chain data, addressing potential concerns over data privacy and cybersecurity.
- o Initial Setup Costs: Although the cloud reduces long-term costs, MSEs may encounter initial expenses related to training, system customization, and data migration.

4. Potential for Industry Transformation

The proposed cloud-based model provides a practical and adaptable solution that can transform the apple agro-industry supply chain. By adopting cloud computing, MSEs can overcome many of the traditional limitations associated with scale, resource constraints, and manual processes. With enhanced data flow, coordination, and market reach, this model can help MSEs grow sustainably and remain competitive. Furthermore, the model's scalability makes it applicable to other sectors within agriculture, presenting opportunities for broader industry transformation.

7.2 Implications for the Agro-Industry

The adoption of a cloud-based supply chain model tailored to the needs of Micro and Small Enterprises (MSEs) in the agro-industry has far-reaching implications that extend beyond operational efficiency. Implementing such a model can reshape how agro-industrial businesses interact, compete, and grow in a rapidly evolving digital economy. This section explores the broader impacts of cloud adoption on the agro-industry and highlights the potential benefits for MSEs, suppliers, distributors, and the industry as a whole.

1. Empowering MSEs with Advanced Technological Access
   Cloud computing allows MSEs to access technologies previously limited to larger companies with significant IT budgets. By providing affordable, scalable, and flexible solutions, the cloud-based model empowers MSEs to operate more competitively, even with limited resources. This increased accessibility to digital tools helps level the playing field, enabling smaller players to optimize their operations and compete in a market dominated by larger businesses.
   - Industry Impact: As more MSEs adopt cloud-based systems, the collective competitiveness of small businesses within the agro-industry improves,

fostering a more diverse and resilient market.
2. Improving Supply Chain Transparency and Collaboration
   The cloud-based model facilitates real-time data sharing and communication across the supply chain, enhancing transparency and building trust among all stakeholders. Suppliers, MSEs, and distributors can seamlessly exchange critical information about inventory, order status, and production schedules, which improves collaboration and coordination. This transparency reduces inefficiencies, minimizes delays, and ensures a smoother flow of goods from farm to market.
   - Industry Impact: Enhanced transparency and collaboration create a more cohesive and integrated agro-industry supply chain, allowing businesses to respond quickly to changes in supply, demand, and market conditions.
3. Reducing Waste and Supporting Sustainability Initiatives
   With real-time data on inventory levels, demand forecasts, and supply needs, the cloud-based model enables MSEs to optimize stock levels, reduce overproduction, and prevent spoilage, especially for perishable goods like apples. By improving inventory accuracy and aligning production with demand, the model minimizes waste, supporting sustainable practices in the agro-industry. Sustainability is increasingly important as consumers seek eco-friendly products, making waste reduction a competitive advantage.
   - Industry Impact: Reducing waste across the supply chain supports environmental sustainability, aligning the agro-industry with global sustainability goals and meeting consumer demand for responsible practices.
4. Enhancing Market Reach and Expanding Customer Base
   Cloud technology opens opportunities for MSEs to expand beyond traditional markets. By facilitating communication

with distributors and providing digital order processing, MSEs can reach a broader audience, including regional and even international customers. This increased market reach helps MSEs diversify their revenue streams, reduce dependency on local markets, and improve financial stability.
    - Industry Impact: Expanded market reach strengthens the economic potential of the agro-industry and enables businesses to cater to diverse customer bases, fostering growth and stability across the sector.
5. Supporting Data-Driven Decision-Making and Innovation
The cloud-based model provides access to data analytics tools that offer insights into supply chain performance, customer preferences, and seasonal demand trends. MSEs can use these insights to make informed, data-driven decisions about production schedules, inventory purchases, and marketing strategies. Access to predictive analytics encourages continuous improvement and drives innovation, as MSEs adapt more effectively to changing consumer demands.
    - Industry Impact: Widespread adoption of data-driven decision-making encourages a culture of innovation within the agro-industry, positioning it as a forward-thinking and adaptable sector capable of meeting modern consumer needs.
6. Mitigating Risks and Building Resilience
With the ability to access real-time data and communicate seamlessly across the supply chain, MSEs can respond quickly to disruptions, such as supply shortages, shifts in demand, or unforeseen events like weather impacts. Cloud technology supports contingency planning by providing MSEs with the flexibility to adjust production, reallocate resources, and coordinate with suppliers and distributors as conditions change.
    - Industry Impact: A more resilient agro-industry is

better equipped to handle external pressures, including market fluctuations and environmental challenges, creating a stable foundation for long-term growth and sustainability.
7. Encouraging a Transition to Digital Ecosystems in Agriculture
The adoption of cloud-based supply chain models encourages a broader digital transformation within the agro-industry. As more businesses adopt cloud solutions, the industry gradually transitions from traditional, manual processes to a digitally connected ecosystem. This shift not only increases operational efficiency but also makes the industry more attractive to investors and talent interested in technology-driven growth.
   o Industry Impact: Digital transformation positions the agro-industry as an innovative and tech-savvy sector, attracting new investment, driving job creation, and fostering digital skills development within the workforce.

7.3 Looking Ahead: Suggestions for Future Development

To further enhance the impact of cloud-based solutions in the agro-industry, additional areas of exploration can help build on this model's foundation, advancing both technology adoption and the effectiveness of supply chain operations. This section offers suggestions for future research and development, focusing on ways to strengthen competitive advantage, optimize system collaboration, and explore innovative applications of cloud technology in agriculture.
1. Exploring Advanced Analytics for Competitive Advantage
Future efforts could focus on integrating advanced analytics and machine learning algorithms to give MSEs deeper insights into market trends, consumer preferences, and

operational efficiencies. Predictive analytics can help MSEs proactively adjust their supply chain, enabling swift responses to changing market conditions and supporting competitive positioning. By developing analytics tools tailored to the agricultural sector, insights can be drawn that drive profitability and promote sustainable practices (Sinha, 2013).

2. Enhancing System Collaboration with Integrated Platforms
Collaboration is essential for a seamless supply chain, yet many MSEs face limitations due to fragmented communication tools. Exploring ways to create fully integrated, cloud-based platforms could unify all aspects of supply chain management, from inventory tracking and order processing to supplier and distributor coordination. Unified platforms with shared dashboards, real-time notifications, and streamlined workflows can facilitate better alignment across the supply chain, fostering responsive and resilient operations (Vidalakis et al., 2011).

3. Incorporating IoT Technology for Real-Time Monitoring
Integrating Internet of Things (IoT) technology with cloud-based systems can enhance monitoring capabilities, especially for perishable goods in sectors like the apple agro-industry. IoT sensors that monitor factors such as temperature and humidity would allow MSEs to maintain optimal storage conditions, reducing spoilage and improving quality control. Cost-effective IoT solutions could provide actionable data on storage and inventory levels, helping small businesses prevent losses while improving operational efficiency.

4. Utilizing Artificial Intelligence for Demand Forecasting
Artificial intelligence (AI) has the potential to improve the accuracy of demand forecasting, enabling MSEs to align production and inventory more closely with market demand.

Research into AI-driven forecasting models that consider variables like weather patterns, consumer trends, and historical data could allow MSEs to optimize inventory levels, reduce waste, and increase profitability. An AI-powered approach to forecasting could make the supply chain more agile and responsive to shifts in demand.

5. Enhancing Cloud Security and Data Privacy

   As cloud computing continues to be adopted, ensuring data security and privacy remains crucial, particularly for MSEs handling sensitive information. Future work could focus on creating secure, tailored cloud environments that protect supply chain data, including customer records, contracts, and financial details. Strong encryption, access controls, and user authentication can reassure MSEs about the security of their data, facilitating wider adoption and building trust in cloud technology (Cook et al., 2011).

6. Developing Cross-Industry Collaboration Models

   The cloud-based model designed for MSEs in the apple agro-industry holds potential for applications in other agricultural sectors. Cross-industry collaboration—where supply chains for different agricultural products, such as fruits, vegetables, and grains, share cloud resources—could improve resource allocation, streamline processes, and foster innovation. This approach can create shared cloud-based ecosystems, enhancing coordination and knowledge sharing among diverse agricultural producers.

7. Adapting Cloud Solutions for Regional and Cultural Needs

   Regional and cultural factors significantly influence the adoption and effectiveness of cloud models. Further research could investigate how cloud-based supply chain solutions can be customized to address the specific cultural, economic, and operational contexts of MSEs across various regions. Tailoring models to accommodate regional practices, digital literacy levels, and infrastructure availability can encourage broader acceptance and maximize the impact of cloud solutions in the agro-industry.

Summary

Future research and development in these areas present numerous opportunities to further support MSEs in the agro-industry. Advancing analytics, enhancing system collaboration, integrating IoT, refining security, and adapting models to regional needs can contribute to a resilient and adaptable digital ecosystem. These developments not only strengthen MSEs' competitive advantage but also foster a collaborative, innovative, and resilient agro-industry capable of thriving in a modern, digitally connected economy.

REFERENCES

Afonso, H., & Cabrita, M. do R. (2015). Developing a Lean Supply Chain Performance Framework in a SME: A Perspective Based on the Balanced Scorecard. *TRIZ and Knowledge-Based Innovation in Science and Industry*, *131*, 270–279. https://doi.org/10.1016/j.proeng.2015.12.389

Agbelusi, J., Arowosegbe, O. B., Alomaja, O. A., Odunfa, O. A., & Ballali, C. (2024). Strategies for minimizing carbon footprint in the agricultural supply chain: Leveraging sustainable practices and emerging technologies. *World Journal of Advanced Research and Reviews*, *23*(3), 2625–2646. https://doi.org/10.30574/wjarr.2024.23.3.2954

Assante, D., Castro, M., Hamburg, I., & Martin, S. (2016). The Use of Cloud Computing in SMEs. *The 7th International Conference on Ambient Systems, Networks and Technologies (ANT 2016) / The 6th International Conference on Sustainable Energy Information Technology (SEIT-2016) / Affiliated Workshops*, *83*, 1207–1212. https://doi.org/10.1016/j.procs.2016.04.250

Bourlakis, M., Maglaras, G., Aktas, E., Gallear, D., & Fotopoulos, C. (2014). Firm size and sustainable performance in food supply chains: Insights from Greek SMEs. *Sustainable Food Supply Chain Management*, *152*, 112–130. https://doi.org/10.1016/j.ijpe.2013.12.029

Dozier, K., & Chang, D. (2007). The Impact of Information Technology on the Temporal Optimization of Supply Chain Performance. *2007 40th Annual Hawaii International Conference on System Sciences (HICSS'07)*, 57–57. https://doi.org/10.1109/HICSS.2007.533

Gardas, B. B., Raut, R. D., & Narkhede, B. (2018). Evaluating critical causal factors for post-harvest losses (PHL) in the fruit and vegetables supply chain in India using the DEMATEL approach. *Journal of Cleaner Production, 199*, 47–61. https://doi.org/10.1016/j.jclepro.2018.07.153

Gokarn, S., & Kuthambalayan, T. S. (2019). Creating sustainable fresh produce supply chains by managing uncertainties. *Journal of Cleaner Production, 207*, 908–919. https://doi.org/10.1016/j.jclepro.2018.10.072

Hill, H. (2001). Small and Medium Enterprises in Indonesia: Old Policy Challenges for a New Administration. *Asian Survey, 41*(2), 248–270. https://doi.org/10.1525/as.2001.41.2.248

Indrajit, R. E., & Djokopranoto, R. (2002). *Konsep Manajemen Supply Chain*. Grasindo.

Kochan, C. G., Nowicki, D. R., Sauser, B., & Randall, W. S. (2018). Impact of cloud-based information sharing on hospital supply chain performance: A system dynamics framework. *International Journal of Production Economics, 195*, 168–185. https://doi.org/10.1016/j.ijpe.2017.10.008

Mahmood, Z. (2011). Cloud Computing for Enterprise Architectures: Concepts, Principles and Approaches. In Z. Mahmood & R. Hill (Eds.), *Cloud Computing for Enterprise Architectures* (pp. 3–19). Springer. https://doi.org/10.1007/978-1-4471-2236-4_1

Montoya-Torres, J. R., & Ortiz-Vargas, D. A. (2014). Collaboration and information sharing in dyadic supply chains: A literature review over the period 2000–2012. *Estudios Gerenciales, 30*(133), 343–354. https://doi.org/10.1016/j.estger.2014.05.006

Priyadarshinee, P., Raut, R. D., Jha, M. K., & Kamble, S. S. (2017). A cloud computing adoption in Indian SMEs: Scale development and validation approach. *The Journal of High Technology Management*

Research, *28*(2), 221–245. https://doi.org/10.1016/j.hitech.2017.10.010

Reyes, J., Mula, J., & Díaz-Madroñero, M. (2023). Development of a conceptual model for lean supply chain planning in industry 4.0: Multidimensional analysis for operations management. *Production Planning & Control*. https://www.tandfonline.com/doi/abs/10.1080/09537287.2021.1993373

Sadegheih, A., Li, D., Sribenjachot, S., & Drake, P. R. (2010). Applying Mixed Integer Programming for Green Supply Chain Management. *The South African Journal of Industrial Engineering*, *21*(2). http://dx.doi.org/10.7166/21-2-46

Sahin, F., & Robinson, E. P. (2007). Flow Coordination and Information Sharing in Supply Chains: Review, Implications, and Directions for Future Research. *Decision Sciences*, *33*(4), 505–536. https://doi.org/10.1111/j.1540-5915.2002.tb01654.x

Simpson, M., Taylor, N., & Barker, K. (2004). Environmental responsibility in SMEs: Does it deliver competitive advantage? *Business Strategy and the Environment*, *13*(3), 156–171. https://doi.org/10.1002/bse.398

Singh, A., Mishra, N., Ali, S. I., Shukla, N., & Shankar, R. (2015). Cloud computing technology: Reducing carbon footprint in beef supply chain. *International Journal of Production Economics*, *164*, 462–471. https://doi.org/10.1016/j.ijpe.2014.09.019

Sinha, A. K. (2013). Opportunities of Cloud Computing in Supply Chain Management. *Anusandhanika*, *V*(I&II), 124–126.

Skintzi, G. (2007). *Supply chain design: An overview* [Unpublish]. https://www.researchgate.net/publication/228993200_Supply_chain_design_an_overview

Tutuhatunewa, A., Surachman, Santoso, P. B., & Santoso, I. (2019). Influence of Information Sharing, Partnership, and Collaboration on

Supply Chain Performance. *Advances in Systems Science and Applications*, *19*(3), Article 3. https://doi.org/10.25728/assa.2019.19.3.689

Wang, M., & Yang, Y. (2022). An empirical analysis of the supply chain flexibility using blockchain technology. *Frontiers in Psychology*, *13*. https://doi.org/10.3389/fpsyg.2022.1004007

Wu, I.-L., Chuang, C.-H., & Hsu, C.-H. (2014). Information sharing and collaborative behaviors in enabling supply chain performance: A social exchange perspective. *International Journal of Production Economics*, *148*, 122–132. https://doi.org/10.1016/j.ijpe.2013.09.016

Yoshino, N., & Taghizadeh-Hesary, F. (2016). *Major Challenges Facing Small and Medium-Sized Enterprises in Asia and Solutions for Mitigating Them* (Working Paper 564). Asian Development Bank Institute (ADBI). http://www.ssrn.com/abstract=2766242

About The Author

Dr. Alfredo Tutuhatunewa, ST., MT. is a lecturer at the Faculty of Engineering at Pattimura University in Ambon, Indonesia. He earned his doctorate in Mechanical Engineering from Brawijaya University in Malang, Indonesia, where he specialized in advancing industrial processes and integrating technology for small and medium enterprises (SMEs) within Indonesia's economic framework. His expertise spans engineering education, supply chain management, cloud computing, and sustainable practices, with a specific focus on applications for the agro-industry.

In this book, Dr. Tutuhatunewa presents a comprehensive framework for applying cloud-based supply chain solutions within the apple agro-industry, specifically aimed at addressing the challenges faced by Micro and Small Enterprises (MSEs). Topics covered include strategies for improving inventory management, enhancing supplier and distributor coordination, and utilizing real-time data sharing to boost efficiency across the supply chain. The book provides insights into leveraging cloud computing to enable MSEs to operate more competitively, reduce waste, and expand market reach. Structured to benefit industry practitioners, academics, and policymakers, this work highlights practical steps toward a digitally transformed, resilient, and sustainable agro-industry.

Prof. Surachman, born on December 8th, 1950. Get a bachelor's degree from the management department of the Brawijaya University, an MSIE degree from the industrial engineering department of ITB, Indonesia, and a doctorate from the management department of the Airlangga University, Indonesia. His field studies are operational management, supply chain management, production planning, total quality control, total quality management. His publications include Cultural shifting of construction workers and the effect on construction project management in East Java (2015), Organizational commitment, and job satisfaction as a mediator the effect of leadership style on OCB of employees (2015), Integration Between Radical Innovation and Incremental Innovation to Expedite Supply Chain Performance Through Collaboration and Open-Innovation: A Case Study of Indonesian Logistic Companies (2018), and The Effect of Corporate Governance and Premium Growth on the Performance of Insurance Companies in Indonesia (2019). Prof. Surachman is currently a professor in management science at the management department of Brawijaya University, Malang, Indonesia.

Purnomo Budi Santoso, Ph.D, born in Yogyakarta on January 13th, 1953. His bachelor's degree was obtained from the UGM mechanical engineering department, Indonesia. A Master's degree was obtained from the University of Aston Birmingham in the field of Computer Aided Design, as well as a Ph.D. from the University of Queensland Australia in the field of Integration of Artificial Intelligence & Database Systems. His fields of study are management information systems, database systems, decision support systems, computer applications, and expert systems. His research includes Intelligent Machine Maintenance Management Information System Engineering for Small and Medium-sized Food Industries (2013), Logistics Management Information System for Fertilizer Distribution PT. Petrokimia Gresik through the integration of cloud computing and Microsoft Office 365 (2013), and the Programming Evaluation and Review Technique (PERT) Model Development on a Phinisi Ship Building Process (2014). Currently, he has retired from the industrial engineering department, Brawijaya University, but his skill is still needed to teach several courses and guide

Masters and doctoral students.

Prof. Imam Santoso, born in Pamekasan, October 5th, 1968. He got a bachelor's degree from Brawijaya University in the field of Agricultural Mechanization, a Master's degree from the Department of Postharvest Technology, Brawijaya University, and a Doctorate from the Department of Agricultural Industrial Technology, Bogor Agricultural Institut. His fields of study are agro-industrial management, agro-industrial risk management, and agro-industrial project development. Some of his publications include Application of FMEA and AHP to formulating the strategy of yogurt production risk (2017), Sugar manufacturing process: risk analysis and mitigation using fuzzy fmea and fuzzy ahp method (2018), A dynamic model for managing adulteration risks of dairy industry supply chain in Indonesia (2018) and Fuzzy sequential model for strategic planning of small and medium scale industries (2019). Prof. Santoso is currently a professor in the Agricultural Technology Department of Brawijaya University, Malang, Indonesia.

www.ingramcontent.com/pod-product-compliance
Lightning Source LLC
Chambersburg PA
CBHW071654240526
45469CB00023B/2376